Songs to Sing to your Cat

and other feline favourites

KRISTINA PATMORE
CAMERON HINDE

"Authors like cats because they are such quiet, lovable, wise creatures, and cats like authors for the same reasons."

- Robertson Davies

SmugCats Press

Text and illustrations © 2017,
Cameron Hinde and Kristina Patmore

ISBN 978-1977837448

Cover design: Cameron Hinde,
assisted by Kristina Patmore

Illustrations: Kristina Patmore
Technical correction: Cameron Hinde

Originated, devised and designed
by Cameron Hinde and Kristina Patmore

twitter.com/_CatSongs

instagram.com/_CatSongs

facebook.com/SmugCats

www.CatSongs.store

To Rupert,
whose forbearance in being routinely
sung to inspired this book.

"I have noticed that what cats most appreciate in a human being is not the ability to produce food - which they take for granted - but his or her entertainment value."

- Geoffrey Household

CONTENTS

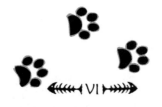

"One cat just leads to another."

- Ernest Hemingway

INTRODUCTION

The habit of singing to one's cat is perhaps as old as the human-feline relationship itself. Indeed, one of the most popular annual festivals of the ancient Egyptians is thought to have involved extensive music, song and dance in honour of the cat-goddess Bast.

How the cat-adoring serenades of these ancient peoples compare to our modern-day bowl-side efforts is not known. Suffice to say, it is likely that our feline cohabiters are as particular now as they were all those centuries ago, and that it is only proper that we make a bit more of an effort for such discerning pals.

Here then, is a collection of songs with which the dedicated cat-person can hope to achieve just that. These songs will, we hope, reduce that predictable tedium of cyclic pacifications (*"I know, I know..."* or *"yes, it really is terribly empty isn't it..."*) as your cat implores you to provide her breakfast. They will also help your cat feel as though her needs are finally being taken more seriously, assuming your performance concludes with a well-filled bowl that is.

Each song comprises original lyrics, carefully researched and constructed to be as attuned as possible to the feline, or feline-worshipping, whim, along with a suggested melody familiar to many. You may, of course, continue to be as creative with words, tune, or lack thereof, as you like, *but only at the discretion of your cat!*

SONGS TO SING TO YOUR CAT

ALL THE PRETTY PUSSCATS

Eleanor Rigby
(All the Lonely People)

Ah look at all the pretty pusscats!
Ah look at all the pretty pusscats!

Baronesss Cupcake, bothering mice
In the shade of a bush, eyes so keen
What has she seen?

Boo in the window, wearing a smile
As he flops on his back in the sun
Warming his tum

All the pretty pusscats
Where do they all come from?
All the pretty pusscats
To them we sing this song!

Professor Biggles, out on patrol
Strutting fences that mark his terrain
He's had a long reign

Sox in the garden, foot in the air
All laid bare, bottom needing a clean
Making a scene

All the pretty pusscats
Where do they all come from?
All the pretty pusscats
To them we sing this song!

Ah look at all the pretty pusscats!
Ah look at all the pretty pusscats!

Kitty and Princess, out playing chess
For control of the street. Who will win
The right to go in?

Rupert the house cat, student of life
As he watches the world down below
Enjoying the show

All the pretty pusscats
Where do they all come from?
All the pretty pusscats
To them we sing this song!

"As a young boy, John doted on the cats.
Every day, he would cycle to Mr. Smith the
fishmonger in Woolton village to buy pieces
of hake for his pets. Later, as a Beatle on
tour, he would phone Mimi to ask how the
cats were getting on without him."

- from Lennon: The Definitive Biography,
by Ray Coleman

"When I play with my cat, who knows if I am not a pastime to her more than she is to me?"

- Michel de Montaigne

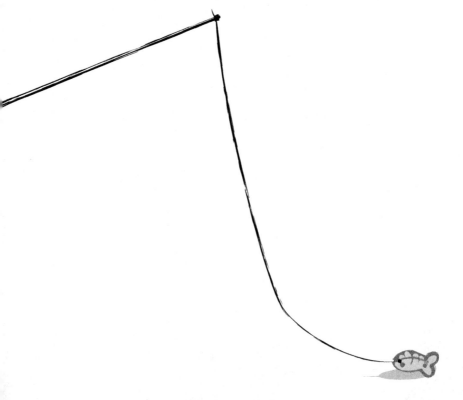

A Pinchful of Catnip

A Spoonful of Sugar

Just a pinchful of catnip makes the pussycat go wild
The pussycat go wild
The pussycat go wild
Just a pinchful of catnip makes the pussycat go wild
In the most exciting way

In every lazy feline's day
There is a need to prompt some play
To propel a pussycat
To show some Oomph!

And as a cat detects the scent
There's a sudden change of bent
A dash! A spree!
A wide-eyed frenzy! 'Cos a

Pinchful of catnip makes the pussycat go wild
The pussycat go wild
The pussycat go wild
Just a pinchful of catnip makes the pussycat go wild
In the most exciting way

GILBERT

John Brown's Body

Gilbert ate his duck and game
And Gilbert ate some ham
Gilbert stole some jellied beef
And Gilbert ate some lamb
Gilbert downed some ageing fish
And then some kibbles too
And Gilbert wondered why Gilbert felt so blue

Glory, glory, bowls of tuna!
Glory, glory, bowls of tuna!
Glory, glory, bowls of tuna!
And the banquet still goes on!

Whoops came up the duck and game
And whoops came up the ham
Whoops came up the jellied beef
And whoops came up the lamb
Whoops came up the kibbles and fish
All over his human's floor
And Gilbert knew that Gilbert wanted more...

BEAUTIFUL

You're Beautiful

My cat is brilliant
My cat is pure
My cat's an angel
Of that I'm sure

She smiled at me from a sunbeam
Stretched out across the floor
Light played across her whiskers
As she flexed a sun-warmed paw...

You're beautiful!
You're beautiful!
You're beautiful, it's true
I saw you flop in a sunny spot
And I can't believe that you
Are a ruthless killer too

11

COME IN

Jolene

Come in, come in, come in, come in
I'm begging of you please to come back in
Come in, come in, come in, come in
Please come in when I rattle and bang this tin

Your beauty is beyond compare
With dainty paws and glossy hair
And whiskers long with eyes of emerald green

With tabby coat like tiger's skin
Your growl speaks of the lion within
But I worry so when you don't come back in

Come in, come in, come in, come in
I'm begging of you please to come back in
Come in, come in, come in, come in
Please come in when I rattle and bang this tin

To know you're safe before I sleep
There's nothing I can do but weep
And cry your name when you don't come back in

And though I know how much at night
You love to prowl and sometimes fight
In my heart I wish you'd rather come back in

Come in, come in, come in, come in
I'm begging of you please to come back in
Come in, come in, come in, come in
Please come in when I rattle and bang this tin

I should have called you earlier
Or held back on your dinner
Now you resolutely will not come back in

My peace of mind depends on you
Been calling you the whole night through
Come home my darling, please just come back in

Come in, come in, come in, come in
I'm begging of you please to come back in
Come in, come in, come in, come in
Please come in when I rattle and bang this tin

"In ancient times cats were worshipped as gods; they have not forgotten this."

- Terry Pratchett

OH, MY PUSS-CAT

Give Me Oil in My Lamp
(Sing Hosanna)

Oh what joy pretty cat, you are purring
Oh what joy pretty cat, you meep
Oh what joy pretty cat, you are meowing
You are meowing that it's time to eat

Oh, my puss-cat; Oh, my puss-cat
Oh, my puss-cat is the King of kings
Oh, my puss-cat; Oh, my puss-cat
Oh, my puss-cat is the King

Oh what joy pretty cat, you are frisky
Oh what joy pretty cat, you prey
Oh what joy pretty cat, you are pouncing
You are pouncing 'cos it's time to play

Oh, my puss-cat; Oh, my puss-cat
Oh, my puss-cat is the King of kings
Oh, my puss-cat; Oh, my puss-cat
Oh, my puss-cat is the King

Oh what joy pretty cat, you are stretching
Oh what joy pretty cat, you mew
Oh what joy pretty cat, you are paddying
You are paddying 'cos it's time to snooze

Oh, my puss-cat; Oh, my puss-cat
Oh, my puss-cat is the King of kings
Oh, my puss-cat; Oh, my puss-cat
Oh, my puss-cat is the King

Mouse Alive!

One Two Three Four Five
Once you caught a mouse alive
Six Seven Eight Nine Ten
Then you let it go again

And where did you let it go?
Right down the back of the kitchen stove!
And why would you put it there?
For the fun of watching us hunt and swear!

THREE IN THE BED

Three in a Bed

There were 3 in the bed
And the big cat said
Roll over, Roll over
So we both rolled over
And he spread out
He stretched a paw
And gave a shout...

Please remember that felines are a noble class
and "King"-size beds are only made for Us!

My Pusscat Sleeps Tonight

Wimoweh
(Mbube)

Sn-oo-OO-oo-OO-oo-OO-oo-OO-oo-OO-oo-oo-oo-ze-away
Sn-oo-OO-oo-OO-oo-OO-oo-OO-oo-OO-oo-oo-oo-ze-away

A-twitch-away, a-twitch-away, a-twitch-away, a-twitch-away
A-twitch-away, a-twitch-away, a-twitch-away, a-twitch-away

A-twitch-away, a-twitch-away, a-twitch-away, a-twitch-away
A-twitch-away, a-twitch-away, a-twitch-away, a-twitch-away

In the armchair, the big old armchair
My pusscat sleeps tonight
Of the jungle, the mighty jungle
My pusscat dreams tonight

18

Sn-oo-OO-oo-OO-oo-OO-oo-OO-oo-OO-oo-oo-oo-ze-away
Sn-oo-OO-oo-OO-oo-OO-oo-OO-oo-OO-oo-oo-oo-ze-away

In the armchair, his big old armchair
His paws all twitch away
Chasing zebra, the grazing zebra
He'll catch them all some day

Sn-oo-OO-oo-OO-oo-OO-oo-OO-oo-OO-oo-oo-oo-ze-away
Sn-oo-OO-oo-OO-oo-OO-oo-OO-oo-OO-oo-oo-oo-ze-away

Hush my pusscat, my darling lion
How big and strong you are
When you're dreaming, so deeply dreaming
A lion's dream afar

*"A cat is a lion in a jungle
of small bushes."*

- Old Indian saying

FELINE FAMILY

The Addams Family Theme

Prrp-prrp-prrp-prrp, scritch scratch
Prrp-prrp-prrp-prrp, scritch scratch
Prrp-prrp-prrp-prrp, Prrp-prrp-prrp-prrp
Prrp-prrp-prrp-prrp, scritch scratch

They're cheeky and they're chirpy
Mysterious and quirky
Often a little shirty
The Feline Family

They keep themselves so cle-an
And hide so we can't see 'em
They're twitchy when they dre-am
The Feline Family

Prrp-prrp-prrp-prrp, scritch scratch
(Bop)
Prrp-prrp-prrp-prrp, scritch scratch
(Flop)
Prrp-prrp-prrp-prrp, Prrp-prrp-prrp-prrp
Prrp-prrp-prrp-prrp, scritch scratch
(Gallop)

So grab a bag of catnip
And give that string a tight grip
Let's all enjoy our friendship
With the Feline Family

"Let us be honest; most of us rather like our cats to have a streak of wickedness."

-Beverley Nichols

GOOGLE

My Bonnie

This morning I tried to get work done
This morning I stared at my screen
I took 5 to do something more fun
And found the web's funniest meme...

Google, google
Oh google more "LOLCats" for me, for me
Google, google
Oh google more "LOLCats" for me

My deadline is early tomorrow
My project's not nearly complete
I'm doomed if I don't get a move on
Right after I've checked this next Tweet...

Google, google
Oh google more "cat loaves" for me, for me
Google, google
Oh google more "cat loaves" for me

I spent my whole lunch break on CatTube
It's time that I went back to work
Maybe just one final cat vid
And then I found Grumpy Cat twerk...

Google, google
Oh google "cats twerking" for me, for me
Google, google
Oh google "cats twerking" for me

By hometime I'm well into Reddit
Lolling at r/catsinsinks
Scrolling through hundreds of cat gifs
I dread what my manager thinks

Google, google
Oh google some "Maru" for me, for me
Google, google
Oh google some "Maru" for me

My project has been a disaster
My boss gave me notice to leave
So I'm jobless and counting my pennies
But internet cats help me grieve!

Google, google
Oh google "@MYSADCAT" for me, for me
Google, google
Oh google "@MYSADCAT" for me

CAT CRAZE

We Didn't Start The Fire

Six thousand years ago
Cats in Egypt ruled the show
Sacred mousers, loved as gods
Protected from their foe.
Symbols of poise and grace
Felines were a warrior race
Death to those who smuggle cats
Death to those who cause them woe.

So many in history
Have a feline deity
Persian cats a magic art
Nordic Freya's cat-drawn cart.
Chinese cat god couldn't keep
World order, fell asleep
Passed her duties on to us
So she could play and snooze.

We didn't start the cat craze
We've been fans of purring
Since the world's been turning.
We didn't start the cat craze
Let the whole wide world know
It's an endless cat show.

Cardinal Richelieu's
Cats stopped him feeling blue
Called them all by fancy names
Kept one on his knees.
Cath-e-rine the Great
Long-time Russian head of state
Gave kittens as gifts
To friends from overseas.

Palace filled with pedigrees
Mogs employed on salaries!
Raised them up to rank of 'Guard'
Tasked them to protect the art.
Isaac Newton cat-door
Legend lasts since days of yore!
A door for mum, another one
For her little kitten!

We didn't start the cat craze
We've been fans of purring
Since the world's been turning.
We didn't start the cat craze
Let the whole wide world know
It's an endless cat show.

The 16th president
Had a special feline bent
Lincoln with his cats did talk
Fed them from a golden fork.
Deemed his White House pet
Smarter than his cabinet
Kittens were adopted for
Rescue from the Civil War.

 25

Roll on 1940
Time of uncertainty
Churchill into Number 10
Brings his cat as resident.
Worldwide frontpage headlines:
War of Ruling Felines!
Munich Mouser chased off!
Nelson serves a big boff!

We didn't start the cat craze
We've been fans of purring
Since the world's been turning.
We didn't start the cat craze
Let the whole wide world know
It's an endless cat show.

Garfield, Top Cat
Tom and Jerry, Cat in Hat
Fluffy kitten greetings cards
Cat 'pin up' calendars.
Internet comes along
Hits like a cat bomb!
Cute kittens everywhere
Digital for all to share.

"Nelson will follow his
master shortly to Downing
Street and make a problem
of protocol. How, it is
asked, will the Munich cat
react to Nelson?"

- Washington Post, 1940

Kitten Wars, Nora
I Can Has Cheezburger...
A million views every day!
What is left for me to say?

We didn't start the cat craze
We've been fans of purring
Since the world's been turning.
We didn't start the cat craze
Let the whole wide world know
It's an endless cat show.

CHANNELLING THE FELINE VOICE

Jellied Meat and Fish

Auld Lang Syne

Should my breakfast be forgot
I'll be sure to let you know!
Should my breakfast be forgot
Ex-pect a morning show!

For jellied meat and fish, my dear
For jellied meat and fish
My heart will cry from crack of dawn
For jellied meat and fish

I'm crying for my pilchards!
I'm crying for my lamb!
I'm crying for a bowl of cream
And a giant leg of ham!

For jellied meat and fish, my dear
For jellied meat and fish
My heart will cry from crack of dawn
For jellied meat and fish

I'll do my best to wake you up
Give your toes a little chew
Jump around your weary head
The mornings you will rue

For jellied meat and fish, my dear
For jellied meat and fish
My heart will cry from crack of dawn
For jellied meat and fish

And when at last you grimly stir
I know my work is done
We each endure a private pain
As kitchenwards we run

For jellied meat and fish, my dear
For jellied meat and fish
My heart will cry from crack of dawn
For jellied meat and fish

And soon we both return to sleep
And enjoy the tranquil calm
And so we share a moments bliss
Until your first alarm!

For jellied meat and fish, my dear
For jellied meat and fish
My heart will cry from crack of dawn
For jellied meat and fish

"Loud cheeps the mouse,
when the cat's no rustling"

- Scots proverb

31

*"You bring me hope, you make me laugh
- and I like it
You get away with murder, so innocent
But when you throw a moody you're all
claws and you bite
That's alright!"*

- From the song 'Delilah',
by Freddie Mercury

I WANT TO GO OUT

I Want to Break Free

I want to go out
I want to go out
I want to get out of this house
To go out on patrol, in the morning
I've got to get out!
You know, You know I need to get out!

It's started to rain
It's started to rain in the garden
Why do you do this to me?!
It's started to rain!
You know! You know it drives me insane!

It's strange, but it's true
I'm gonna to stay in
And spend some time with you
Because I want to be sure
When I walk out that door
I'll have the sunshine on me, yeah
I need the sunshine on me!
Oh won't the sun shine on me?!

The rain still goes on
I can't get used to, staying inside, staying inside
Staying inside more!
Such a bore!
Gotta have a chance to roam, hey
You know, I can't be stuck at home
You better sort it out!
'Cos I got to go out!

Kitty Litter Footie

Hokey Cokey
(Hokey Pokey)

You put your right paw in
Scoop some litter out
In, Out, In, Out
Spread it all about!
You do the Litter Footie and you turn around
That's what it's all about...

Woah! Kitty Litter Footie
Woah! Kitty Litter Footie
Woah! Kitty Litter Footie
Paw stretched, toes spread, scoop scoop scoop!

You put your left paw in
Scoop some litter out
In, Out, In, Out,
Kick it all about!
You do the Litter Footie and you turn around
That's what it's all about...

Woah! Kitty Litter Footie
Woah! Kitty Litter Footie
Woah! Kitty Litter Footie
Paw stretched, toes spread, scoop scoop scoop!

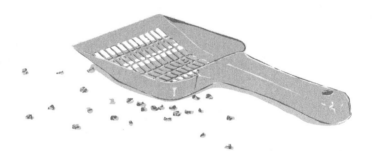

VETS TODAY

Yesterday

Yesterday all my troubles seemed so far away
Now I'm going to the vets today
Oh, how I yearn for yesterday

Suddenly, carry case is in front of me
Seeing it makes me want to flee!
Oh, vets today, not where I want to be!

Why we have to go, I don't know, they didn't say
I did nothing wrong, now I hate the vets today!

Yesterday I could gladly eat and sleep and play
Now I have no place to hide away
Oh, how I fear the vets today

Why we have to go, I don't know, they didn't say
I did nothing wrong, now I long for yesterday!

Snooze Around the House

Rock Around the Clock

One two three o'clock, four o'clock snooze
Five six seven o'clock, eight o'clock snooze
Nine ten eleven o'clock, twelve o'clock snooze
I'm gonna snooze around the house tonight!

So smooth out that paper in a shaft of sun
I'm gonna have a rest when the clock strikes one

I'm gonna snooze around the house tonight
I'm gonna snooze snooze snooze in broad daylight
I'm gonna snooze, gonna snooze around the house tonight!

When the clock strikes two, three and four
Draped on a chair and stretching a paw

I'm gonna snooze around the house tonight
I'm gonna snooze snooze snooze in broad daylight
I'm gonna snooze, gonna snooze around the house tonight!

When the chimes ring five, six and seven
I'm twitching my paws in kittycat heaven

I'm gonna snooze around the house tonight
I'm gonna snooze snooze snooze in broad daylight
I'm gonna snooze, gonna snooze around the house tonight!

When it's eight, nine, ten, eleven too
I'll be snug on the sofa next to you

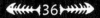

I'm gonna snooze around the house tonight
I'm gonna snooze snooze snooze in broad daylight
I'm gonna snooze, gonna snooze around the house tonight!

When the clock strikes twelve to sleep you head
You know I'll already have your bed

I'm gonna snooze around the house tonight
I'm gonna snooze, gonna snooze around the house tonight!

"Kittens are born with their eyes shut. They open
them in about six days, take a look around,
then close them again for the better part of their
lives."

- Stephen Baker

Claws

These Boots Are Made for Walkin'

You keep claiming you've got something on me
Shouting loudly "NO!", but you are fools
Warnings unheeded, your furnishin's are unshielded
So now I'm start'n to sharpen up my tools

These claws are made for scratchin'
And that's just what they'll do
One of these days these claws are gonna
Scratch that sofa too

You keep beratin', n' threat me with a wet sprayin'
Yellin' if you catch me flexin', my paw
I'm just toyin', so I'm gonna do some destroyin'
And what's mine is mine n' that rug is mine for sure

These claws are made for scratchin'
And that's just what they'll do
One of these days these claws are gonna
Scratch that carpet too

You tried citrus to stop my cuttin' edge business
You don't respect my deconstructive flair
And you keep prayin', I'll desist my flayin'
Of that heirloom antique rosewood table and chair

These claws are made for scratchin'
And that's just what they'll do
One of these days these claws are gonna
Scratch that dresser too.

Are you ready claws? Start scratchin'!

"A rose has thorns, a cat has claws;
certainly both are worth the risk."

- proverb

THE PUSSERCAT SONG

The Lumberjack Song

I'm a pussercat, and I'm okay
I work all night and I work all day

He's a pussercat, and he's okay
He sleeps all night and he sleeps all day

I climb up trees
I shout for lunch
I go to the lavatory
Some days I go out hunting
And bring home gifts for tea

He gets stuck up trees
We feed him lunch
We clean his litter tray
When he comes home from hunting
We clean up in dismay

He's a pussercat, and he's okay
He sleeps all night and he sleeps all day

I catch a bird
I eat it whole
I wander down the street
I visit other food bowls
To see what's there to eat

He catches moths
He eats them whole
He wanders down the street
He visits other food bowls
To see what's there to eat?!

He's a pussercat, and he's okay
He sleeps all night and he sleeps all day

I patrol the road
I guard the fence
I visit number two
They give me plates of tuna
And named me Malibu

He patrols the road
He guards the fence
He visits number two?
He gets plates of tuna
And they've named him Malibu?!

He's a pussercat, and he's okay
He sleeps all night and he sleeps all day

I chew some grass
I throw it up
I visit seventeen
They offer me smoked salmon
And call me their Little Queen

He chews some grass
He throws it up
He visits seventeen?!

What's this?
Visits number seventeen?! Oh, My!
And I thought he was our Snooper!

He's a pussercat, and he's okay
He sleeps all night and he sleeps all day

He's a pussercat and he's OKAAAAAAY!
He sleeps all night and he sleeps all day!

44

I'M HERE!

From Out the Battered Elm Tree
(Cuckoo Song)

Beside the empty food bowl a cat cries out "I'm here!"
As from the busy kitchen, no human seems to hear.

I'm here, I'm here, I'm here, I'm here, I'm here!
I'm here, I'm here, I'm here, I'm here, I'm here!

*"Cats seem to go
on the principle
that it never does
any harm to ask
for what you
want."*

- Joseph Wood Krutch

KITTEN IT'S WET OUTSIDE

Baby it's Cold Outside

I want to go out...	...But, Kitten, it's wet outside
I want to go and play...	...But, Kitten, it's wet outside
I think that I have seen...	...Soon you'll be wanting back in
...some tasty mice!	I'll hold the door, it's not so nice

The rain is such a worry...	...Do I have to hold this all day
I'm gonna sit behind this door...	...But you were so keen before
But Mummy I'm in no hurry...	...Darling, please do scurry
Well, maybe I'll just wash my paw...	...Holding the door, that's all I'm for

Mummy it's so cold...	...Yes, Kitten, you'd freeze out there
Rain will wet my coat...	...It's just five degrees out there
Maybe I'll use the sand...	...Must I really wait and stand?
No, I think we agree...	...Agree it's inside we should be

We'll try again later today...	...Close the door and walk away
Or maybe check at the other door?...	...Don't be silly, hear the fire-place roar!
I guess I could sleep...	...On the sofa, in the heat

Because it's wet
Because it's wet outside

Stroke your Cat

Row your Boat

Stroke stroke stroke your cat
Daringly on the tum
Claws out
Feet kick
Cuddles are such fun!

Scratch scratch scratch your cat
Gently on the head
Perks up
Runs away
Time now to be fed!

DISEMBOWELMENT RHAPSODY

Bohemian Rhapsody

Is this a blood stain?
I hope it's imaginary!
What are these entrails
What have you brought to me?

I've brought you a gift!
What do you think it'll be?
I'm just a small Puss!
You must be so proud of me!

Well I'm searching high, searching low
What have you caught, where did it go?

Isn't it exciting!?
Let me tell you of my deed, my deed...

Mama! Just caught a mouse
Put my teeth around its head
Flashed my claws, now it's dead!
Mama, it was just the one
But I've left it on your pillow all the same!

Mama, meeaow!
Didn't mean to make it die...

I sometimes wish you'd never go out at all!
Move Along! Move Along!
This really is disgusting.

Oh look! It's still alive!
Saw it twitching, now it's mine!
What fun I'll have with it this time!

Get out! Crazy Cat! You've got to go!
You've covered my bed in blood and guts
And gore!

Mama, meeaow!! I don't want to go...
Oh Look!
The mouse has hidden behind the door!!

I saw a little silhouetto of a mouse Get the mouse Get the mouse Where'd the bloody mouse go?!	I saw a little silhouetto of a mouse Tasty mouse Tasty mouse Where'd the Tasty mouse go?!

Hope it's not all mangled!

Give it a little dangle!

SQUEAK!!!

Get-the-cat-out! Get-the-cat-out!
Get-the-cat-out! Get-the-cat-out!
Get-the-cat-out!

Let-me-go!
MEAEW-eaew-eaew!
I'm just a poor puss,
nobody loves me

So you think you can stop me by shutting me out?
Well you know I'll just scream, kick and shout?!

Oh, Meeaow! Can't do this to me, Meeaow!
Just let me back in! Just let me back in right now!

Oh wow...
I'm feeling shattered
Maybe we should sleep.
Stretched out on the sofa
The mess doesn't matter to me

Oh meow...
I'm feeling shattered
Maybe we should sleep.
Curled up by your knees
The mouse doesn't matter to me

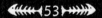

INDEX BY TUNE

"I had been told that the training procedure with cats was difficult. It's not. Mine had me trained in two days."

- Bill Dana

ABOUT THE AUTHORS

This book was written by two hopeless cat fanatics with the help of Rupert, our rather large and fluffy Siberian forest cat. We humans have been singing together with our cats (rather haphazardly) for many years and it finally felt like time to organise, refine and share some of our musical creations with fellow cats and cat lovers.

Visit us at
catsongs.store
for more about Rupert, us, or the songs in this book.

Printed in Great Britain
by Amazon